THE LEAF AND
THE CLOUD

Other Books by Mary Oliver

THE LEAF AND
THE CLOUD

Other Books by Mary Oliver

MARY OLIVER

THE LEAF AND THE CLOUD

DA CAPO PRESS

The quotation from "Symposium" is from *The Great Dialogues of Plato* by Plato, translated by W. H. D. Rouse, copyright © 1956, renewed 1984 by J. C. G. Rouse. Used by permission of Dutton Signet, a division of Penguin Putnam, Inc. All other acknowledgments can be found on page 55.

A CIP catalog record for this book is available from the Library of Congress.
ISBN 0-306-80993-1

Published by Da Capo Press
A Member of the Perseus Books Group
http://www.perseusbooksgroup.com

1 2 3 4 5 6 7 8 9   03 02 01 00

For

Molly Malone Cook

We have seen that when the earth had to be prepared for the habitation of man, a veil, as it were, of intermediate being was spread between him and its darkness, in which were joined, in a subdued measure, the stability and insensibility of the earth, and the passion and perishing of mankind.

But the heavens, also, had to be prepared for his habitation.

Between their burning light,—their deep vacuity, and man, as between the earth's gloom of iron substance, and man, a veil had to be spread of intermediate being;—which should appease the unendurable glory to the level of human feebleness, and sign the changeless motion of the heavens with a semblance of human vicissitude.

Between the earth and man arose the leaf. Between the heaven and man came the cloud. His life being partly as the falling leaf, and partly as the flying vapour.

—John Ruskin
From *Modern Painters*, vol. V, part VII, ch. 1

CONTENTS

THE LEAF AND
THE CLOUD

Flare

1.

Welcome to the silly, comforting poem.

It is not the sunrise,
which is a red rinse,
which is flaring all over the eastern sky;

it is not the rain falling out of the purse of God;

it is not the blue helmet of the sky afterward,

or the trees, or the beetle burrowing into the earth;

it is not the mockingbird who, in his own cadence,
will go on sizzling and clapping
from the branches of the catalpa that are thick with blossoms,
   that are billowing and shining,
      that are shaking in the wind.

2.

    You still recall, sometimes, the old barn on your great-grandfather's farm, a place you visited once, and went into, all alone, while the grownups sat and talked in the house.

It was empty, or almost. Wisps of hay covered the floor, and some wasps sang at the windows, and maybe there was a strange fluttering bird high above, disturbed, hoo-ing a little and staring down from a messy ledge with wild, binocular eyes.

Mostly, though, it smelled of milk, and the patience of animals; the give-offs of the body were still in the air, a vague ammonia, not unpleasant.

Mostly, though, it was restful and secret, the roof high up and arched, the boards unpainted and plain.

You could have stayed there forever, a small child in a corner, on the last raft of hay, dazzled by so much space that seemed empty, but wasn't.

Then—you still remember—you felt the rap of hunger—it was noon—and you turned from that twilight dream and hurried back to the house, where the table was set, where an uncle patted you on the shoulder for welcome, and there was your place at the table.

3.

Nothing lasts.
There is a graveyard where everything I am talking about is,
now.

I stood there once, on the green grass, scattering flowers.

4.

Nothing is so delicate or so finely hinged as the wings
of the green moth
against the lantern

against its heat
against the beak of the crow
in the early morning.

Yet the moth has trim, and feistiness, and not a drop
     of self-pity.

Not in this world.

     5.

My mother
was the blue wisteria,
my mother
was the mossy stream out behind the house,
my mother, *alas, alas,*
did not always love her life,
heavier than iron it was
as she carried it in her arms, from room to room,
oh, unforgettable!

I bury her
in a box
in the earth
and turn away.
My father
was a demon of frustrated dreams,
was a breaker of trust,
was a poor, thin boy with bad luck.
He followed God, there being no one else
he could talk to;
he swaggered before God, there being no one else
who would listen.

Listen,
this was his life.
I bury it in the earth.
I sweep the closets.
I leave the house.

6.

I mention them now,
I will not mention them again.

It is not lack of love
nor lack of sorrow.
But the iron thing they carried, I will not carry.

I give them—one, two, three, four—the kiss of courtesy,
    of sweet thanks,
of anger, of good luck in the deep earth.
May they sleep well. May they soften.

But I will not give them the kiss of complicity.
I will not give them the responsibility for my life.

7.

Did you know that the ant has a tongue
with which to gather in all that it can
of sweetness?

Did you know that?

8.

The poem is not the world.
It isn't even the first page of the world.

But the poem wants to flower, like a flower.
It knows that much.

It wants to open itself,
like the door of a little temple,
so that you might step inside and be cooled and refreshed,
and less yourself than part of everything.

9.

The voice of the child crying out of the mouth of the
    grown woman
is a misery and a disappointment.
The voice of the child howling out of the tall, bearded,
    muscular man
is a misery, and a terror.

10.

Therefore, tell me:
what will engage you?
What will open the dark fields of your mind,
    like a lover
        at first touching?

11.

Anyway,
there was no barn.
No child in the barn.

No uncle no table no kitchen.

Only a long lovely field full of bobolinks.

12.

When loneliness comes stalking, go into the fields, consider
the orderliness of the world. Notice
something you have never noticed before,

like the tambourine sound of the snow-cricket
whose pale green body is no longer than your thumb.

Stare hard at the hummingbird, in the summer rain,
shaking the water-sparks from its wings.

Let grief be your sister, she will whether or no.
Rise up from the stump of sorrow, and be green also,
    like the diligent leaves.

A lifetime isn't long enough for the beauty of this world
and the responsibilities of your life.

Scatter your flowers over the graves, and walk away.
Be good-natured and untidy in your exuberance.

In the glare of your mind, be modest.
And beholden to what is tactile, and thrilling.

Live with the beetle, and the wind.

This is the dark bread of the poem.
This is the dark and nourishing bread of the poem.

Work

1.

I am a woman sixty years old and of no special courage.
Everyday—a little conversation with God, or his envoy
    the tall pine, or the grass-swimming cricket.
Everyday—I study the difference between water and stone.
Everyday—I stare at the world; I push the grass aside
    and stare at the world.

The spring pickerel in the burn and shine of the tight-
    packed water;
the sweetness of the child on the shore; also, its
    radiant temper;
the snail climbing the morning glories, carrying
    his heavy wheel;
the green throats of the lilies turning from the wind.
This is the world.

Comes the hunter under the red leaves;
come the hounds, on their stubbies;
like wind they pour through the grass,
like wind they pour up the hill;
like wind they twist and swirl in the long grass.

Everyday—I have work to do:

I feel my body rising through the water
                not much more than a leaf;
and I feel like the child, crazed by beauty
                or filled to bursting with woe;
and I am the snail in the universe of the leaves
                trudging upward;
and I am the pale lily who believes in God,
                though she has no word for it,

and I am the hunter, and I am the hounds,
and I am the fox, and I am the weeds of the field,
and I am the tunnel and the coolness under the earth,
and I am the pawprint in the dust,
I am the dusty toad who looks up unblinking
and sees (do you also see them?) the white clouds
in their blind, round-shouldered haste;

    I am a woman sixty years old, and glory is my work.

    2.

The dreamy heads of the grass in early summer.
In midsummer: thick and heavy.
Sparrows swing on them, they bend down.
When the sparrow sings, its whole body trembles.

Later, the pollen shakes free.
Races this way and that way,
like a mist full of life, which it is.
We stand at the edge of the field, sneezing.
We praise God, or Nature, according to our determinations.

Then the grass curls or breaks, or we cut it.
What does it matter?
Do you think the grass is growing so wild and thick
    for its own life?
Do you think the cutting is the ending, and not, also,
    a beginning?
This is the world.

The pink globes of the peonies
open under the sun's early-morning hands.

The vine of the honeysuckle
perks upward—
the fine-hold of its design
did not need to be so wonderful, did it?
but is.

This is the world.

The bat squeaks.
The bat leans down out of dark July
with his elf's face.

The twenty-winged cloud of yellow butterflies
floats into the field.
The mustard-heads bend under their soft weight.

This is the world.

    3.

Would it be better to sit in silence?
To think everything, to feel everything, to say nothing?

This is the way of the orange gourd.
This is the habit of the rock in the river, over which
   the water pours all night and all day.
But the nature of man is not the nature of silence.
Words are the thunders of the mind.
Words are the refinement of the flesh.
Words are the responses to the thousand curvaceous moments—
   we just manage it—
   sweet and electric, words flow from the brain
   and out the gate of the mouth.

We make books of them, out of hesitations and grammar.
We are slow, and choosy.
This is the world.

      4.

All day I have been pining for the past.
That's when the big dog, Luke, breathed at my side.
Then she dashed away then she returned
in and out of the swales, in and out of the creeks,
her dark eyes snapping.
Then she broke, slowly,
in the rising arc of a fever.

And now she's nothing
except for mornings when I take a handful of words
and throw them into the air
so that she dashes up again out of the darkness,

like this—

this is the world.

5.

The green pea
climbs the stake
on her sugary muscles.

The rosy comma of the radish
fattens in the soil.

Farmers call to the white oxen, together they pull the plow.
Girls sigh upward against the bodies of young men.
The century plant opens at last in the frail moonlight.

6.

And how shall we speak of love
except in the splurge of roses, and the long body
    of the river
shining in its silk and froth;

and what could be more wonderful
than the agility and the reaching of the fingers of Hannah,
who is only seven days old;

and what could be more comforting than to fold grief
like a blanket—
to fold anger like a blanket,
with neat corners—
to put them into a box of words?

7.

It may be the rock in the field is also a song.
And it may be the ears of corn swelling under their
    green sleeves
are also songs.
And it may be the river glancing and leaning against
    the dark stone is also a deliberate music.

So I will write my poem, but I will leave room for the world.
I will write my poem tenderly and simply, but
    I will leave room for the wind combing the grass,
for the feather falling out of the grouse's fan-tail,
    and fluttering down, like a song.

And I will sing for the bones of my wrists,
    supple and exemplary.
And the narrow paths of my brain, its lightnings and issues,
    its flags, its ideas.
And the mystery of the number *3*.

I will sing for the iron doors of the prison,
and for the broken doors of the poor,
and for the sorrow of the rich, who are mistaken and lonely,

and I will sing for the white dog forever tied up in the orchard,
and I will sing for the morning sun and its panels
    of pink and green on the quiet water,
and for the loons passing over the house.

I will sing for the spirit of Luke.
I will sing for the ghost of Shelley.
I will sing for the Jains and their careful brooms.

I will sing for the salt and the pepper in their little towers
    on the clean table.
I will sing for the rabbit that has crossed our yard
    in the moonlight,
stopping twice to stamp the cold ground
    with his narrow foot.

I will sing for the two coyotes who came at me with
    their strong teeth
and then, at the last moment, began to smile.

I will sing for the veil that never lifts.
I will sing for the veil that begins, once in a lifetime,
    maybe, to lift.
I will sing for the rent in the veil.
I will sing for what is in front of the veil, the
    floating light.
I will sing for what is behind the veil—
    light, light, and more light.

This is the world, and this is the work of the world.

From The Book of Time

1.

I rose this morning early as usual, and went to my desk.
But it's spring,

and the thrush is in the woods,
somewhere in the twirled branches, and he is singing.

And so, now, I am standing by the open door.
And now I am stepping down onto the grass.

I am touching a few leaves.
I am noticing the way the yellow butterflies
move together, in a twinkling cloud, over the field.

And I am thinking: maybe just looking and listening
is the real work.

Maybe the world, without us,
is the real poem.

2.

For how many years have you gone through the house
    shutting the windows,
while the rain was still five miles away

and veering, o plum-colored clouds, to the north,
away from you

and you did not even know enough
to be sorry,

you were glad
those silver sheets, with the occasional golden staple,

were sweeping on, elsewhere,
violent and electric and uncontrollable—

and will you find yourself finally wanting to forget
all enclosures, including

the enclosure of yourself, o lonely leaf, and will you
dash finally, frantically,

to the windows and haul them open and lean out
to the dark, silvered sky, to everything

that is beyond capture, shouting
I'm here, I'm here! Now, now, now, now, now.

3.

I dreamed
I was traveling

from one country
to another

jogging
on the back
of a white horse
whose hooves

were the music
of dust and gravel
whose halter
was made of the leafy braids

of flowers,
whose name
was Earth.
And it never

grew tired
though the sun
went down
like a thousand roses

and the stars
put their white faces
in front of the black branches
above us

and then
there was nothing around us
but water
and the white horse

turned suddenly
like a bolt of white cloth

opening
under the cloth-cutter's deft hands

and became
a swan.
Its red tongue
flickered out

as it perceived
my great surprise
my huge and unruly pleasure
my almost unmanageable relief. . . .

4.

"'Whoever shall be guided so far towards the mysteries of love, by
contemplating beautiful things rightly in due order, is approaching the last
grade. Suddenly he will behold a beauty marvellous in its nature, that very
Beauty, Socrates, for the sake of which all the earlier hardships had been
borne: in the first place, everlasting, and never being born nor perishing,
neither increasing nor diminishing; secondly, not beautiful here and ugly
there, not beautiful now and ugly then, not beautiful in one direction and
ugly in another direction, not beautiful in one place and ugly in another
place. Again, this beauty will not show itself like a face or hands or any
bodily thing at all, nor as a discourse or a science, nor indeed as residing
in anything, as in a living creature or in earth or heaven or anything else,
but being by itself with itself always in simplicity; while all the beautiful
things elsewhere partake of this beauty in such manner, that when *they* are
born and perish *it* becomes neither less nor more and nothing at all
happens to it. . . .'"

5.

What secrets fly out of the earth
when I push the shovel-edge,
when I heave the dirt open?

And if there are no secrets
what is that smell that sweetness rising?

What is my name,
o what is my name
that I may offer it back
to the beautiful world?

Have I walked
long enough
where the sea breaks raspingly
all day and all night upon the pale sand?

Have I admired sufficiently the little hurricane
of the hummingbird?

the heavy
thumb
of the blackberry?

the falling star?

6.

Count the roses, red and fluttering.
Count the roses, wrinkled and salt.
Each with its yellow lint at the center.

Each with its honey pooled and ready.
Do you have a question that can't be answered?
Do the stars frighten you by their heaviness
  and their endless number?
Does it bother you, that mercy is so difficult to
  understand?
For some souls it's easy; they lie down on the sand
  and are soon asleep.
For others, the mind shivers in its glacial palace,
  and won't come.
Yes, the mind takes a long time, is otherwise occupied
than by happiness, and deep breathing.
Now, in the distance, some bird is singing.
And now I have gathered six or seven deep red,
  half-opened cups of petals between my hands,
and now I have put my face against them
and now I am moving my face back and forth, slowly,
  against them.
The body is not much more than two feet and a tongue.
Come to me, says the blue sky, and say the word.
And finally even the mind comes running, like a wild thing,
  and lies down in the sand.
Eternity is not later, or in any unfindable place.
Roses, roses, roses, roses.

      7.

Even now
I remember something

the way a flower
in a jar of water

remembers its life
in the perfect garden

the way a flower
in a jar of water

remembers its life
as a closed seed

the way a flower
in a jar of water

steadies itself
remembering itself

long ago
the plunging roots

the gravel the rain
the glossy stem

the wings of the leaves
the swords of the leaves

rising and clashing
for the rose of the sun

the salt of the stars
the crown of the wind

the beds of the clouds
the blue dream

the unbreakable circle.

Riprap

1.

Upon the rocks grow beautiful, small things.
Mussels, with mossy beards.
Dark blue shells.

They sigh as the tide rises.

Starfish cruise and cling.
Bluefish plunge and leap, their long bodies swirl,
    their teeth are uncountable.
The tides rise, the blue sprawl and polish climbs the rocks
    and is momentarily held there.
The loggerhead with her pink parrot's head
    feasts among the mussels.
Daylight descends slowly, and the *now* that is a day
    becomes the *now* that is the night,
the white moon the only boat,
the white heron the only fisherman left on the black rocks.

2.

In my mind, the arguers never stop—
the skeptic and the amazed—

the general and the particular, in their
    uneasy relationship.

Then the robin sings.

Then the bulb of the lily becomes the stalk,
the stalk opens into a handkerchief of white light.

O what is beauty
that I should be up at
four A.M. trying to arrange this
thick song?
What is beauty that I should
bow down in the fields of the world, as though
someone, somewhere,
made it?

O, what is beauty
that I feel it to be so hot-blooded and suggestive,
so filled with imperative

beneath the ease of its changes,
between the leaves and the clouds of its thousand
    and again a thousand opportunities?

        3.

The sweet-faced cat,
the good goat,
the golden feet of the hen—
    the sealed jug of her egg—

the black mole's long-knuckled hands,
the spears of the grass,
    the sun on everyone's back, yours and mine.

Also the poem on the page,
also the painting on the white wall;
also the instruments and the arms holding them
    and the voices issuing from them.

The turnip, the cabbage, the crook-necked squash;
the three blue bowls;
the fork and the knife.

The sailboat,
the dragger swaying above its heavy nets,
the pink dory crossing the bay with two boys and a dog.

I'm never sure
which part of this dream is me
and which part is the rest of the world.

Therefore.

    4.

Every morning I wake, dress in the dark, go downstairs.
I look out of every window.
I go out and stand on the lawn.
In the east, the slightest light begins
    flinging itself upward
and my heart beats (never an exception) with excitement.
(My gratitude to you, dear heart!)

Though it will all vanish utterly, and surely in
    a little while,
I know what is wonderful—
I know what to hoard in my heart more than the value
    of pearls and seeds.
There was the day you first spoke my name.
There was a white house at the edge of the harbor.
There was the swan, and the hummingbird.
There was music, and paper, and the tirelessly pursued work.
There were a thousand and again a thousand unforgettable days.

And still I'm looking at everything—
in the wide morning and the strike of noon
I'm humming, and clapping my hands,
and I can't stop
not for any reason
not even for the easiest thought.

And, anyway, what is thought
but elaborating, and organizing?
What is thought
but doubting, and crying out?

     5.

(In the dark, in the distance,
I can just see the heron
dimpling then calming her long wings.)

     6.

As reliable as anything you will ever know,
time moves its dim, heavy thumb over the shoreline

making its changes, its whimsical variations.
Yes, yes, the body never gets away from the world,
its endless granular shuffle and exchange—

everything is one, sooner or later—
the red fox and the bullrush,
the industrious ant and the sleepy bear,
the green crab and the minnow,
the pink boat and the dog in the pink boat,

Shelley's body and the gleaming sand.

When the praying mantis opens its wings
    it becomes a green flower.
When the egg breaks
    it becomes a bird.
When the river is finished, its avenues of light
fold and drop and fall into
and become the sea.

Therefore.

        7.

But what is it then that sits in my heart,
that breathes so quietly, and without lungs—
that is here, here in this world, and yet not here?

        8.

Does the body have a soul?
Does the weedy mussel clinging to the rocks have
    a soul?

Does the black snake, sliding along, perking up
the black lump of its head, does it have a soul?

The body has a soul.

What about the butterfly, the tree root?

The butterfly, the tree root.

Is the wren proof?
And the bed of new lilies just opening,
all silk and spit, is it also proof?

The wren, and the lilies.

Does the grain of sand
know it is a grain of sand?
Will secrets fly out of me
when I break open?
Are the stars standing
in any order?
Is supplication
useful?

Exactly.

9.

Now, in the dark, the white heron
strokes the air over the salt marsh, then she

dangles the forks of her feet and her long legs and comes
floating down to the rocks. She shakes herself, just once,

so that her body for an instant is a white fire—
not herself but the perfection of self,

a white fire.
If I look carefully I can see it.

Then the yellow eye moves, she arches forward slightly
and stares into the moving water,

     10.

and we are back
in this world.

Rhapsody

1.

Gold bead after hot gold bead formed
   on the green tassels until they were
the crest of summer, yellow and orange
   seed-casks, skull-curls, tight, bright,
one might even say rhapsodic—oh!
   the sweetness of reality!

Later I caught him, Time hurrying by, by
   the blue sleeve, and I harangued him
against his foolish claim, that the field is all his,
   that everything is his.

Not so. I was there. In the honey-land.
   And you were there too.
I was there with you.

2.

My brother the fox
goes home to his home
under the red roses.

The muskrat
sinks
with a rippling happiness
in the dark water.

(He has sharp teeth, the color of corn.
Though once he did me great harm
I forgive him.
And hope he forgives me.)

The bluebird
is dropping the pearls of his song
out of the sky.

The ant
is sleeping
inside his pale
delicately tunneled hill.

    3.

I am so busy among
Shelley's long poems, Plato, Godwin's
Enquiry, Carlyle concerning
the failed revolution that bloody sorrow, and,
as always, Emerson.

Now and again, of course, I look up; a person must.
Maybe I eat an apple or a pear.
Maybe I walk out with the happy dogs.
Maybe I come back into the house, calling your name.

Or maybe you whisper mine.

4.

Have you seen the roses shiver then open their small fluted
    perfect panels of mildest silk, besieged
by another idea? Have you seen their wild faces
    when they first open?

Have you seen them lifting themselves to the
    heat of the sun,
or the rain tapping with its slender fingers on
    the pale sand below?
Or the bunched bee in the blossoms, doing its work,
    entering and emerging, and the flowers
shining in their bed of leaves?

5.

Bless the fingers,
for they are as darting as fire.
Bless the little hairs of the body,
for they are softer than grass.
Bless the hips
for they are cunning beyond all other machinery.
Bless the mouth
for it is the describer.
Bless the tongue
for it is the maker of words.
Bless the eyes
for they are the gifts of the angels,
for they tell the truth.
Bless the shoulders
for they are a strength and a shelter.

Bless the thumb
for when working it has godly grip.
Bless the feet
for their knuckles and their modesty.
Bless the spine
for it is the whole story.

6.

Because there is no substitute for vigorous and exact
description, I would like to say how
your eyes, at twilight, reflect, at the same
time, the beauty of the world, and its crimes.

7.

If you are in the garden, I will dress myself in leaves.
If you are in the sea I will slide into that
smooth blue nest, I will talk fish, I will adore salt.
But if you are sad, I will not dress myself in desolation.
I will present myself with all the laughters I can muster.
And if you are angry I will come, calm and steady, with
some small and easy story.

Promises, promises, promises! The tongue jabbers, the heart
strives, fails, strives again. The world is perfect.
Love, however, is an opera, a history, a long walk, that
includes falling and rising, falling and rising, while
the heart stays as sweet as a peach, as radiant and
grateful as the deep-leaved hills.

Gravel

1.

When death
carts me off to the bottomlands,
when I begin
the long work of rising—

Death, whoever and whatever you are, tallest king of
tall kings, grant me these wishes: unstring my bones;
let me be not one thing but all things, and wondrously
scattered; shake me free from my name. Let the wind, and
the wildflowers, and the catbird never know it. Let
time loosen me like the bead of a flower from its wrappings
of leaves. Let me begin the changes, let me—

Can you imagine a world without certainty?
The wind rises the wind falls.

        The gravels of the world,
        the stones of the world
        are in their proper places.

The vast, writhing
worms of the sea
are in their places.

The white gulls
on the wet rocks
are in their places.

All is certainty.

    2.

Ben sluices through the ferns, hound-smart.
The bracken up to his neck.
He breaks from the wood and gallops over the field.
The sass of his voice rises—

> (Death that slow swim,
> death that long walk over the dunes,
> death that bleached clamshell . . .)

and the rabbits scatter.

> (Oh, heart, I would not dangle you down into
>   the sorry places,
> but there are things there as well
>   to see, to imagine.)

    3.

Even the mosquito's
   dark dart,

flashing and groaning;
   even the berries, softening back
into the black bog;
   even the wood duck's
white-circled eye,

and the first white lilies
on the shaggy pond,

and the big owl, shaking herself
out of the pitchpines,

even the turtle scratching in the dust,
even the black ant, climbing the mile-high hill,

even the little chattering swift
diving down into the black chimney.

Everything is participate.
Everything is a part of the world
   we can see, taste, touch, hold onto,

and then it is dust.
Dust at last.
Dust and gravel.

(In the distance, the rabbit-field.
Ben—his face in the grass, his chomping.
His sweet, wild eyes.)

4.

Are you afraid?
    The ear of corn knows whereof it is plucked.

Are you afraid?
    The wind moves this way and that way, something
        is pushing it.

Are you afraid?
    Somewhere a thousand swans are flying
        through the winter's worst storm.

They are white and shining, their black beaks
    open a little, the red tongues flash.

Now, and *now,* and *now,* and *now* their heavy wings
    rise and fall as they move across the sky.

5.

Goodbye to the goldfinches
in their silver baskets.
Goodbye to the pilot whales, and the curl of their spines
in the crisp waves.
Goodbye to the grasshopper.
Goodbye to the pond lilies, the turtle with her
cat's head.
Goodbye to the lion's mane floating in the harbor
like a spangled veil.

Goodbye to the moon uprising in the east.
Goodbye to the going forth, and coming home.

Goodbye to the going forth, and holding on, and worrying.
Goodbye to the engine of breath.

The knee sings its anguish.
The ears fill with the sound of ringing water.
The muscles of the eyes pull toward sleep.

Goodbye to the swaying trees.
Goodbye to the black triangles of the winter sea.
Goodbye to oranges, the prick of their fragrance.
Goodbye to the fox sparrow,
goodbye to the blue-winged teal.
Goodbye to lettuce, and the pale turnip,
and the gatherings of the rice fields.
Goodbye to the morning light.
Goodbye to the goldfinches
            and their wavering songs.

Slowly
up the hill,
like a thicket of white flowers,
forever
is coming.

         6.

It is the nature of stone
to be satisfied.
It is the nature of water
to want to be somewhere else.

Everywhere we look:
the sweet guttural swill of the water
tumbling.
Everywhere we look:
the stone, basking in the sun,

or offering itself
to the golden lichen.

It is our nature not only to see
that the world is beautiful

but to stand in the dark, under the stars,
or at noon, in the rainfall of light,

frenzied,
wringing our hands,

half-mad, saying over and over:

what does it mean, that the world is beautiful—
what does it mean?

The child asks this,
and the determined, laboring adult asks this—

both the carpenter and the scholar ask this,
and the fisherman and the teacher;

both the rich and the poor ask this
(maybe the poor more than the rich)

and the old and the very old, not yet having figured it out,
    ask this
desperately

standing beside the golden-coated field rock,
or the tumbling water,
or under the stars—

what does it mean?
what does it mean?

     7.

The high-piled plum-colored storm-heavy clouds
are approaching.
The fly mumbles against the glass.

This is the world.

The hot little bluebirds in the box are getting ready to fly.
This is the world.

The sweet in the parsnip
waits for our praise.

The dragonfly lives its life
without a single error, it also
waits for our praise.

The pale-green moths are pressing
against the screen, fluttering, they are
dying to get in to press their papery bodies
into the light.

This is the world.

8.

Listen, I don't think we're going to rise
in gauze and halos.
Maybe as grass, and slowly.
Maybe as the long-leaved, beautiful grass

I have known, and you have known—
or the pine trees—
or the dark rocks of the zigzag creek
    hastening along—

or the silver rain—

or the hummingbird.

9.

I look up
into the faces of the stars,
into their deep silence.

10.

This is the poem of goodbye.
And this is the poem of don't know.

My hands touch the lilies
then withdraw;

my hands touch the blue iris
then withdraw;

and I say, not easily but carefully—
the words round in the mouth, crisp on the tongue—

dirt, mud, stars, water—
I know you as if you were myself.

How could I be afraid?

Evening Star

1.

Once
in the woods
snake came
like a whip
like a piece of a circle
like black water
flowing down the hill.
"Watch me,"
it whispered—
then poured
like black water
through the field—
then hurried down,
like black water,
into the mouse's hole.

And out of this
you might draw
the thinnest of shining threads—

whirl it around and
fling it into the air,
fling it into the air—

again and again it will land on the earth
crimped and cursive,
but spelling nothing,

for, dear God,
we too are down here
in such darkness.

    2.

It is easy to fall down on your knees
when the shining rain begins to happen.

It is easy to be thankful
for the bundles of wild roses
ledged along the dune.

It is as easy as if you were yourself a flower in the field,
    the rain tossing you and tossing you,

until you are that flower—
    as torn as muddy as golden as that.

    3.

The snake never shuts its eyes.

    4.

I have lit candles.
    (Though I am not ready, I am willing.)

I have placed one word next to another
  to build something full of praise.
I have admired the hummingbird, dazzling among the lilies.
Also the tooth of the otter, the compost pile,
  the first star in the evening sky.
    (Though I am not ready, I am simmering.)

        5.

And certainly and easily I can see
how God might be one rose bud,
one white feather in the heron's enormous, slowly opening wing.

It's after that
it gets difficult.

        6.

The snake never shuts its eyes.
The mouse sits tight.

        7.

The good shepherd of the fields, whoever he is,
has so many wonderful and saucy tricks.

I want to find him,
I want to discover just one more trick.

Oh, nobody runs so hard
as the doubters running over the hot fields,

crying out for faith,
looking for it in the high places and the low places,
looking for it everywhere,

oh, see how I run!

8.

The snake never shuts its eyes.
The mouse sits tight
in the beautiful field.

9.

I went down all alone, to the black pond.
Slow summer day.
No one around.
Not even a bird singing, not a wind awake, nothing.

Yet nothing could ever convince me
that I was alone.

If God exists he isn't just butter and good luck—
he isn't just the summer day the red rose,

he's the snake he's the mouse,
he's the hole in the ground,

for which thoroughness, if anything, I would adore him,
if I could adore him.

Adore him.

10.

The first streak of light in the darkness,
the first bird to sing,
the first whale to rise out of the black water,
the first morning of the spring tide
the first lupine geranium poppy
first sweet corn,
the first afternoon spent outdoors, after illness,

first child
speaking its first words
first peach on the tree
first grapes
first hand-holding   first kiss

first afternoon of snow
flakes like salt tapping the leaves
then the swirl then the soft clouds tumbling down

first road to the ocean,
first smell of the ocean
first white heron
first abalone,

first crab, iridescent in the seaweed
first mountain
first fern
first egg with a tapping from inside

first rose
red rose   first white rose   opening
itself and no more than itself

and more than itself.

11.

The pickerel
swims up from the pond from its roses of slow decay, and
looks at me
astonished.

What is it I need to know?

The gypsy moths, still caterpillars,
wrench themselves from the milky shreds of birth
and set out on the long journey
in the shining tree.

What is it I don't know that I need to know?

12.

Think of me
when you see the evening star.
Think of me when you see the wren
    the flowing root of the creek beneath him,
    dark   silver   and cold

Remember me I am the one who told you
he sings for happiness.
I am the one who told you
that the grass is also alive, and listening.

alleluiah alleluiah
sighs the pale green moth
on the screen door,

alleluiah alleluiah
the red tongues of the white swans
shine out of their black beaks
as they shout
as their wings rise and fall

rise and fall

oh rise and fall

through the raging flowers of the snow.

ACKNOWLEDGMENTS

My thanks to the editors of the following magazines, in which sections of this poem have previously appeared.

DoubleTake: From The Book of Time
Five Points: Evening Star
The Ohio Review: Riprap
Shenandoah: Flare
The Southern Review: Work
The Virginia Quarterly Review: Gravel

"Flare" received the 1998 James Boatwright III Prize for Poetry; my thanks to *Shenandoah*.

"Flare" also appears in *The Best American Poetry 1999*, published by Scribner.

"Work" also appears in *The Best American Poetry 2000*, published by Scribner.

And my deepest appreciation to the Lannan Foundation for their gift of a 1998 Lannan Literary Award.